Card Player

HOW TO WIN

AT

ONLINE POKER

Card Player
HOW TO WIN
AT
ONLINE POKER

BARRY SHULMAN
WSOP EUROPE MAIN EVENT CHAMPION

CARDOZA PUBLISHING

Thanks go to:
• Michael Wiesenberg for encouraging me to write this needed book and then editing the text. Much of the glossary comes from his *Official Dictionary of Poker*.
• My son Jeff ("Happy") for discussing poker theory with me almost daily and verifying content. Jeff also oversees everything at *Card Player* Media, including this project.
• Diego Cordovez for discussing every single concept with me, and then reading, editing, correcting and enhancing the document.
• Wendy Chang for her art and design work.
• Dominik Karelus and Justin Marchand for turning electronic text into a real book.
• My wife Allyn for indulging me while I wrote the copy when I was supposed to be on an around-the-world vacation.

Cardoza Publishing is the foremost gaming publisher in the world with a library of more than 200 up-to-date and easy-to-read books and strategies. These authoritative works are written by the top experts in their fields and with more than 10,000,000 books in print, represent the most popular gaming books anywhere.

ISBN 13:978-1-5804-2323-6
ISBN 10:1-5804-2323-X
Library of Congress Control Number: 2014939766

About the Author

Barry Shulman, the 2009 *World Series of Poker Europe* Main Event champion—he defeated Daniel Negreanu heads-up for the title—is a winner of more than $4.5 million in live tournament earnings. A two-time gold bracelet winner at the WSOP and winner of millions more at cash tables, he is one of the most accomplished Texas hold'em tournament players today. He has cashed in well over 100 major poker tournaments.

Barry is also one of the most powerful and influential figures in the poker world. He is the chairman of Card Player Media, publisher of *Card Player,* the oldest-running and most widely read poker magazine (more than 500,000 circulation monthly), which is published in twenty-five languages around the world. He is the author of two terrific books, *52 Tips for Limit Hold'em Poker* and *52 Tips for No-Limit Hold'em Poker.*

Barry has expanded his online presence with several websites. CardPlayer.com is the largest and most informative poker portal in the world, while CardPlayerPokerSchool.com is one of the best free poker-training sites.

Shulman is also known for his high-end worldwide travel and can be followed at JetSetWay.com. Or, better yet, join him for hosted travel at JetSetWayVacations.com.

TABLE OF CONTENTS

INTRODUCTION • 11

OVERVIEW OF WINNING ONLINE • 13

GENERAL CASH GAME STRATEGY • 44

MULTITABLE TOURNAMENT STRATEGY • 50

MULTITABLE TOURNAMENT STRATEGY: MORE TIPS • 65

MULTITABLE TURBO TOURNAMENT STRATEGY • 83

SIT-AND-GO STRATEGY • 91

HYPER-TURBO STRATEGY • 106

TOOLS AND TRAINING • 111

FINAL TIP • 118

GLOSSARY • 119

INTRODUCTION

This book focuses on how to win online, or if you are already a winning player, how to win more.

This book fills a long neglected void. Plenty of good books exist on how to play poker, addressing the needs of beginners, intermediates, and expert players. But few books have been published about *online* poker. This is ironic, because right now there are more poker games running online than in all the **brick-and-mortar**—those with a physical, as opposed to a virtual, presence—casinos and cardrooms in the world.

And there is a lot more variety of games and limits online. Not only no-limit hold'em but also pot-limit Omaha, Omaha 8-or-better (a split-pot game), limit hold'em, several varieties of draw poker (both high and low), new games such as Badugi, and many other games run around the clock at virtually every online poker site.

You can also find tournaments of all kinds, from heads-up sit-and-gos all the way up to megatournaments with tens of thousands of participants. No land-based cardroom offers all these varieties. You can find games online at stakes in which players can win and lose hundreds of thousands—even millions—of dollars in a single session all the way down to penny-stakes poker. And all online poker sites offer games for play money, in which you can learn how to play without having to risk real money. No brick-and-mortar cardroom offers penny stakes games or play money games. They can't afford to.

This book is written for those who are just learning to play poker, those who are making the transition from land-based cardrooms to online games, and those who already have skills and just want to improve them.

OVERVIEW OF WINNING ONLINE

GENERAL ADVICE

The rules for poker games online are the same as anywhere else. In a showdown, the best hand still wins. If one player makes a bet on any round that no one else calls, the bettor wins. But most importantly, in the long run a skillful player wins.

When you play online, you do not have two key tools that you are accustomed to using in a brick-and-mortar setting: visual and verbal cues. You can, of course, learn something from what players type into the chat box, but this is not nearly as powerful as what players say—or don't say—during a live game.

But you gain one extremely powerful weapon: a plethora of information about your opponents. To accumulate this information, you have access to a multitude of tools and information not available to brick-and-mortar players. To become a successful online player, you absolutely must use these additional weapons.

You must become familiar with and take advantage of the following:

- Online Site Selection
- Frequent Player Points and Bonuses
- The Main Lobby
- Notes on Players
- Software Tools (including hand-tracking applications)
- Online Tells
- Multitabling

> **Note**
> Unless otherwise noted, much of the discussion in this book assumes that the game of choice is no-limit hold'em. This is because no-limit hold'em is the most popular form of poker, both online and off. Due to its popularity, you'll find the greatest selection of games in this form of poker, and therefore you'll also find the greatest number of players that you can beat.

TIP #1

ONLINE PLAYERS PLAY DIFFERENTLY

When you compare poker in brick-and-mortar (B&M) cardrooms with poker online, the game is the same, but *play* is different. There are several reasons for this, not all necessarily related:

- There are no visual clues as to what a particular bet means. You can't see what another player is doing when he bets or calls, so **tells**, a mannerism that gives away your holdings, take a different form.

- Players are generally younger. They have grown up on Internet-based interactive games, and as a group are usually wilder and more aggressive than their elders.

- In most cases, every player has a hidden identity. Some high-profile players play under their own names or their pseudonyms are widely known, but most players play in anonymity.

- You see more stupid bets and bad calls in online games because there is little fear of embarrassment—due to anonymity.

- The stakes are often small enough online that some participants do not care whether they win or lose. Players who might play solidly in a live game don't take the game seriously when they are playing for much smaller stakes than usual.

- Online players have many distractions when playing at home. The player who just called a huge all-in bet with a hand that cannot win may have just heard his kids shrieking and inadvertently clicked the wrong button.

- Many online players play multiple tables at once. Some players play up to twenty-four simultaneous games, which makes it impossible for them to pay attention to any single table.

- Online games tend to have a different style compared to land-based games. You will see more **probe bets** (in a no-limit game, a small bet made to see if anyone will raise or to determine who will just call), smaller opening raises, lighter preflop reraises, and more multiway pots. If you are used to playing in brick-and-mortar games you will need to adjust to the tendencies of online players.

- Many players use player tracking software to gather data on their opponents and on themselves. These tools have a lot of implications—it's important to know how to make adjustments against opponents who use these programs and it's important to use them yourself (when permitted by your online poker site) to analyze and improve your own play.

One thing that comes out of all of this is that it's easy to play poorly online and nobody will be the wiser (except for yourself). Take advantage of your opponents' poor play and be careful not to fall into the same traps that will hurt your own play.

One big difference from B&Ms is that players online are more **aggressive**, which means more action, a style of play characterized by much betting, raising, and reraising. When hold'em was first expanding from Nevada to other venues, many good players had difficulty making the transition from Las Vegas to California B&Ms. In California, the players were much more aggressive and more willing to call with slim holdings. This was a difficult adjustment for many of the Las Vegas **rocks**, extremely tight (conservative) players who play only premium cards, who thought they would find a **berry patch**—a game full of weak players, one that is easy to beat—in the Golden State. Similarly, many players find it difficult to transition from live play to online. The real issue is that many do not know how to adjust properly to a different style.

Another related difference is that higher-stakes no-limit games in B&Ms tend to be more aggressive than low limit games. This is not necessarily true online, particularly when comparing medium-limit online games to higher limits. Once you get into online games bigger than the very small ones with blinds of $1 and $2, the games don't necessarily get more aggressive as they get larger. Another way of putting this is that the small medium games are just as aggressive as the large medium games. (The very large games, called **nosebleed limits**, are another type of animal, one that this book won't be discussing.)

Because of the lack of audio and visual clues, there are lots of probe bets. You must both learn about and use probe betting to hone your online skills. Don't make the mistake of overbetting when you are just probing. But also don't make the mistake of automatically folding whenever your small bet is raised.

TIP #2

YOU CAN WIN—AND WIN MORE—ONLINE

- Game selection is much better online than in any brick-and-mortar casino. There are so many more tables that it's easy to find games in which you are the best player. Finding these games is by far the easiest and surest way to be a winning poker player.

- The rake is usually far less per hand online than in casinos. The large number of competing poker sites online combined with lower infrastructure costs means that you pay less to play online.

- You play way more hands per unit of time online than in land-based games. A casino game might typically play anywhere from twenty-five to thrity-five hands per hour. Online, you'll usually get 100 to 150 hands each hour. And **multitabling**, playing at more than one table at a time, enables you to increase the number of hands exponentially, so you can conceivably play thousands more hands every hour. The more hands per hour you play as a winning player, the more money you earn.

- You give yourself a chance for a huge return on your money because you can find tournaments with enormous fields, sometimes up to 50,000 players. The return on investment when you eventually get lucky and make a score in one of these tournaments will be massive.

- You can actually play for free online and with "frequent player points" awarded for such play earn your way into actual cash events.

- When you play online, there is no tipping or travel time and expense. Those are significant portions of a live player's budget.

- All of the preceding means that you can play lower stakes online than you would in a land-based cardroom, without reducing your earnings. By playing many more hands per hour at lower stakes you can significantly reduce your variance without sacrificing income, which means that your bankroll requirements are significantly reduced.

TIP #3

CHOOSE AN ONLINE POKER SITE
WITH A LARGE SELECTION OF GAMES

Play in a room with a deep pool of players and a wide variety of games. More choices means more chances of finding players and games that you can beat.

TIP #4

MAKE SURE YOU EARN FREQUENT PLAYER POINTS AND BONUSES

One of the draws to a specific poker site is its frequent player points program or its **bonuses** (such as deposit bonuses or other promotions). It's possible for a break-even player, or even a player who loses a little, to make a profit purely from frequent player points and bonuses.

Frequent player points are like airline miles. They are awarded to build loyalty. You earn them, so use them. Remember that they have value.

TIP #5

STUDY THE MAIN LOBBY CAREFULLY

The main **lobby** is your entry into an online cardroom. It is the primary source of information about all the games available on the site. The lobby summarizes every game that is running—what type of game, what stakes, the number of players at each table, as well as average pot size, average stack size, average number of players seeing the flop, the number of hands played per hour, and the names of every player at each table.

CardPlayer *THE POKER AUTHORITY*

Table	Game	Stakes	Players	Wait	Avg Pot	Players/Flop	Hands/Hr
Opal	Hold'em	$.05/.10	4/10	0	$2.13	53%	>99
Mount Char	Hold'em	$.25/.50	6/6	0	$6.50	50%	62
Farma	Hold'em	$.25/.50	6/6	1	$4.55	41%	80
Heat	Hold'em	$.05/.10	10/10	0	$1.77	35%	75
La Quinta	Hold'em	$.25/.50	10/10	3	$3.79	32%	>99
Merida	Hold'em	$1/2	10/10	1	$11.36	27%	>99
Glendale	Hold'em	$.05/.10	7/10	0	$2.01	26%	>99
Silver State	Hold'em	$.25/.50	5/10	0	$4.11	21%	>99
Jade	Hold'em	$2/4	3/10	0	$26.21	19%	>99

Main Lobby with Tables Sorted by
Percentage of Players Seeing Flop

You can and must use this information to pick the best tables to play. No brick-and-mortar cardroom gives you this information. You usually have to join a game without knowing much about the players in that game, and you never have the amount of choices that you have online.

So when you enter the lobby, don't just sign up for the first available seat. Look around first. Filter the list to show games with specific characteristics. Select your best table by criteria such as: the number of players seated, games with lots of pots played, average size of each pot, percentage of players taking the flop, and so on. When a specific game is highlighted (by clicking on the table) you'll see information about the players. displayed. Read the notes you have about those players and, if you've color-coded them, see whether they are solid, loose, dangerous or whatever else you deem important.

| Lobby | Account | Cashier | Options | Security | Languages | Requests | Help |

C∂rd Player — THE POKER AUTHORITY

Room Name	Game	Stakes	Players	Wait	Ave Pot	Plrs/Flop	Hnds/Hr
Opal	Hold'em	$.25/.50	10/10	0	$190	41%	49
Mount Char	Hold'em	$.25/.50	10/10	0	$16.50	50%	62
Farma	Hold'em	$.25/.50	10/10	1	$77.30	33%	80
Heat	Hold'em	$.05/.10	6/6	0	$4.20	35%	75
La Quinta	Hold'em	$.25/.50	6/6	3	$1.75	100%	>99
Merida	Hold'em	$1/2	6/6	1	$8.50	0%	0
Glendale	Hold'em	$.05/.10	2/2	0	$31.10	46%	>99
Silver State	Hold'em	$.25/.50	1/10				
Jade	Hold'em	$2/4	1/6				

Table: Mount Charleston

Find Player   BigDonk

Looking for an Opponent that you want to play against

Don't just blindly pay attention to your own game. Keep watching the lobby and change (or add) tables when it's best for you.

Online cardrooms have cash games and tournaments. The most certain way to win is to play with worse players, no matter the game format. Keep referring to notes and using other criteria to pick games with weaker players. Finding worse players has less relevance in multitable tournaments (which are described later) because you can't select your tablemates there. But you can assume that as buy-ins go up, skill level and focus generally go up too.

TIP #6

TAKE AND USE NOTES WISELY

Online poker sites have easy-to-use tools that enable you to write and keep notes on each of your opponents. Take as many notes on other players as possible. This might be difficult when you are multitabling, but it is worth it to play fewer tables so that you can accumulate as much information as possible. This information will help you to win more overall.

For example, you could be faced with a large bet on the river and would ordinarily not call with a marginal hand, but if your notes tell you that this particular player often makes a large bluff in this situation, you may make a winning call that you would otherwise not have considered.

Flag players with written notes and color code them. For example, loose-passive **calling stations**—weak players who rarely raise, but call almost every bet—can be colored green, weak-tight players blue, maniacs red, and so on. It's very important to know your opponents. With all the hands you'll be playing, and particularly if you multitable, you will see thousands of different players. There's no way you can remember how they all play, and you often won't have much time to observe them before having to make an important decision.

Something specific to look for: If you see a player suddenly act very differently from his normal behavior, he probably has a very strong or a very weak hand. Add this to your notes and the next time you see that behavior you may know what it means.

It's just as important to keep notes about how other players perceive *you*. If you try a big bluff that fails it is likely that your opponent will remember it or make his own note about it, which is something you need to make a note of and factor into your play against that particular opponent next time that you play against him. Any time that you make an unusual play against an opponent you should make a note about it since it will likely influence how that player plays against you in the future.

TIP #7

BUY AND USE SOFTWARE TOOLS

If you want to be a winning online player, you *must* use these tools. Other players are using them and you are at a significant disadvantage if you don't also employ them. Specifically, I am referring to third-party tracking software. Many of your opponents know how you play. To make it a level playing field, you need information about how *they* play. These applications allow you to keep track of hands that you play (which you can use to find your own tendencies and flaws) and the hands other people play with you. You can't get the secrets (like what they have if they fold), but you can get important data such as how often they raise or call, how aggressive they are, whether they raise or call with specific hands such as ace-king, and dozens of data points that will help you in future hands.

You can't remember all these things about all players or even about yourself. However, you can buy software that does just that for you. Hold'em Manager and PokerTracker are two such applications. Both provide **heads-up displays (HUDs)** that appear next to each player on your screen with statistics about their play. Each application provides a wealth of information; You customize the software to decide which statistics to display.

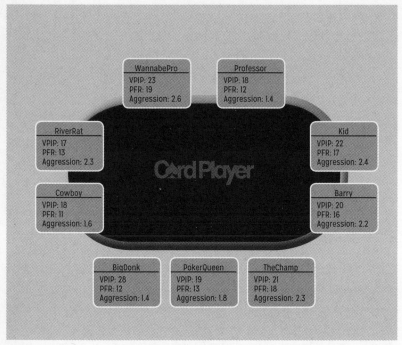

Using HUD Software to Review Information about Opponents

This information is important both for the beginner who has not honed his observation skills and the advanced player who is multitabling and needs to know about opponents' tendencies at a glance. We'll go into more detail about tools later.

Tools do not, however, replace notes; they supplement them. Notes provide you with information that tracking software cannot, such as whether a particular player tends to go **on tilt**, playing poorly and irrationally due to emotional upset, after losing a big hand.

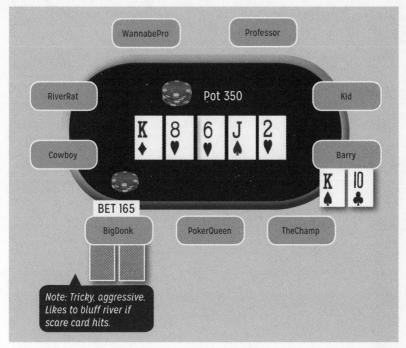

Using Notes to Review Information about Opponents

So what do you do with all this information? You categorize players by their tendencies and then play different players differently:

- **Tight aggressive players**: Generally stay away from them; at least be very careful.

- **Maniacs**: Usually try to **isolate**—bet in such a way, usually by raising or reraising enough to make it difficult for others to come into the pot—and trap them.

- **Rocks**: Raise rocks more often to steal their blinds, but don't get cute if they call. That is, if they push back then back off unless you make a hand likely better than theirs; don't continue trying to buy the pot.

- **Bluffers**: As with maniacs, against habitual bluffers the best strategy is often to check and call.

- **Calling stations**: **Value bet** (bet a hand with the intention of getting called by a lesser hand, as opposed to getting your opponent to fold) and **overbet** (bet more than you think would be called by a typical player or more than the situation calls for).

TIP #8

LOOK FOR ONLINE TELLS

Although you can't see your opponents, you can still find tells. The most important are the speed with which an opponent does or does not act, and betting amount. Other tells include chat box remarks, taking the big blind, and checkbox (advanced action button) usage.

The following tips illustrate a few examples.

TIP #9

SPEED OF OPPONENT'S ACTION GIVES YOU INFORMATION

A long delay followed by a big bet or a raise often means a big hand, not unlike a sigh followed by a bet or raise in live action. But be careful. A delay may be due to a multitabler's attention to another game or a connection problem. Use a long delay as an indicator, something to be sensitive to. Be aware—from your notes, of course!—if the behavior is a habit or an aberration for the player.

A long delay followed by a check often means no improvement, but the player is trying to convey the impression that he has a big hand. He often just doesn't want you to bet. This doesn't necessarily mean it's a safe time to bluff. He may call anyway; it's just that he's trying to discourage your bet. Similar to the preceding, for some players, a long delay followed by a check may be an attempt at a reverse tell—that is, the player is just waiting to check-raise with a big hand. Again, your notes will help you in these situations.

Similarly, a quick check or bet, if consistent with a particular player, has meaning. Sometimes it means the player just improved and sometimes it means that he did not improve. Pay attention! In general, though, bluffs in no-limit games are more often made quickly or after a short pause.

TIP #10

WATCH THE CHAT BOX FOR TELLS

Remarks in the chat box are similar to audible tells. You can't hear the intonation, so you don't get information by that means, but what a person types (when faced with a bet or having just made a bet) often directly correlates to the strength of his hand. Some people turn off the chat box entirely, but this is a mistake.

I turn off announcements from the poker room that have nothing to do with me, but keep an eye out for my opponents' chat.

People can hide behind their true identities and say things they would never say in person. Anger comes out as does abusiveness. These can be good tells that a person is on tilt, which may affect his play. He'll make bigger bets than he would normally, enter more pots, go after specific players, call more than he usually does, and so on. If you sense than an opponent is on tilt, it is often a good time to call him more liberally and to value bet more often (with larger amounts) while bluffing less.

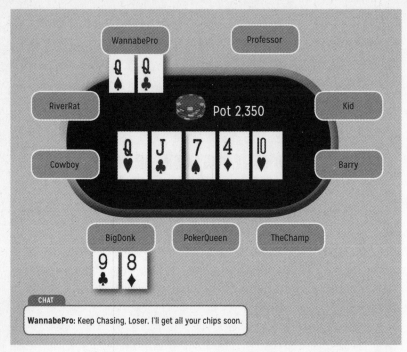

Monitor Chat for Players that may be Tilting

TIP #11

KEEP AN EYE ON THE BIG BLIND FOR TELLS

In a casino, it makes sense to post the big blind when you sit down if the button is just to your left, particularly in a 10-handed game, because it may take several minutes before you get to play a hand.

Not waiting for the big blind in an online game may indicate a lack of discipline, which may be a clue to how that individual plays in general. It just doesn't take too long for the blind to reach you online.

My advice: Wait for the blind. In fact, you may even want to wait an extra round just to pick up some preliminary information on how others are playing. Just don't wait too long. Most poker sites automatically remove a player from the table for missing multiple blinds in a row, usually three.

TIP #12

LOOK FOR CHECK BOX UTILIZATION TELLS

How a player, particularly an unsophisticated one, uses **check boxes** (controls that permit a player to select an action before it is his turn to act), can be an indication of the strength of his hand. It's easy to spot when a player has used advance action boxes because his action are instantaneous, faster than a human could click.

Perhaps the most useful tell is the "check" check box being used. Often an instant check (indicating that the advanced action box was utilized) means a weak or drawing hand.

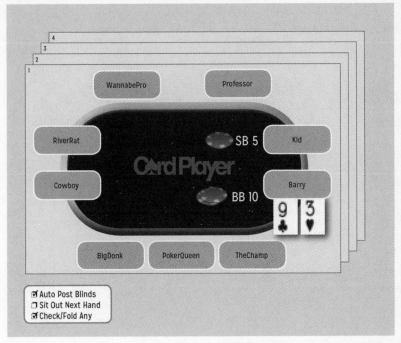

Using the 'Fold' Advanced Action Button

Only use check boxes to your advantage. If you are multitabling and want to fold, it is okay to check the "fold" box and move along. But rarely should you use the other check boxes.

And if you're ever lucky enough to catch an opponent using the "call any" check box, it's most likely someone on a draw after the flop or, better yet, a moron. Someone who flopped a set might also use this check box. But if you're ever sure someone is using it and you have the nuts, just bet your whole stack.

And of course, never use the feature yourself.

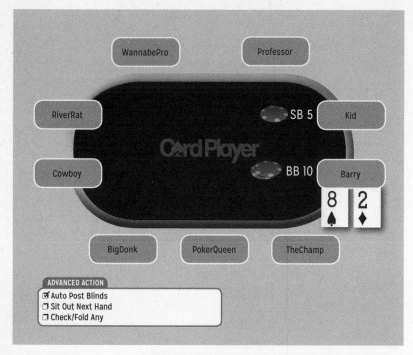

Advanced Action Buttons that are Available to the Big Blind

Three check box options appear when you have the big blind: "check," "check/fold," and "call any/check." Watch for opponents who use the first two options. When someone **limps**, opening the pot on the first round of betting by calling the big blind (and not raising), he almost assuredly holds weak cards, particularly if at other times the big blind pauses before doing acting. It's unusual for an opponent to use "call any/check," but you can take advantage of that as described earlier.

If you know that a player uses the "fold in turn" check box when you have the small blind or button you can just **min raise**, raising the minimum amount possible, to get the player to fold. There is no reason to risk more.

One other check box to be aware of is the "call [*amount*]" check box, where *amount* is whatever the total bet is at that point. If a player instantly calls a small bet, you know that he checked that box and also likely does not have a great hand. If you know that someone regularly uses this check box and the betting gets to him and he does not instantly respond, he likely has a good hand—or at least an unusual hand (could be a bluff).

You certainly know he doesn't have something that can be handled with an automatic response.

TIP #13

BETTING AMOUNTS GIVE AWAY IMPORTANT INFORMATION

Betting amount tells fall into the category of pattern tells. Many players always come in for the same raise, say two-and-a-half times the big blind. This gives away little. But others vary their opening, and the amount often correlates to their holdings. If so, make a note for future reference. Some players over-raise with middle pairs. Some min raise with a big hand; some with a weak hand, yet one that warrants a raise.

Some always **three-bet** (reraise an opening raise) in late position with whatever hand they were going to play anyway while others always raise or reraise with ace-king but not big pairs. Keep track.

TIP #14

LEARN ABOUT MULTITABLING

Players can play in more than one game at once. That ability provides advantages for both the multitablers and those who play against them.

You can show multitabling on the screen in various ways. If just two tables, you can place them side by side and see both at once. Four tables can be handled similarly, although the view into each is a bit smaller. As you add more tables, they overlap. However, even if a window is covered up, it pops to the front when it is your turn to act. Some dedicated multitablers use two or more monitors to more easily keep all tables visible.

When you multitable, you will probably win less at each individual table, but ideally you will win more per hour overall than if you played just one game. Conversely, that means when you play against a multitabler, since he is giving something up, you might be able to win pots from him that you wouldn't if he was playing only one table and giving it his full attention. Except for the very best players, most multitablers make automatic and predictable plays most of the time, and you can counter those situations. Just make sure that you're not playing so many tables that you can't properly react.

Some people play as many as twenty-four games at once. They tend to be young, good players, who play mathematically, use software tools, and play somewhat like robots, albeit smart ones.

Ironically, it makes sense both to be a multitabler and play against multitablers. Start out with one game, then add another, and yet another. When you start losing track of what you're doing it is time to stop adding tables. This is a gradual process to spread over weeks and months, depending on your skill level and also motor skills. Furthermore, multitabling is more stressful than playing just one game, but if you're playing to win and not just to have fun, that's business. This book assumes that your goal is to maximize your win rate.

How to Take Advantage of Multitabling

If multitabling opponents are not maximizing their own return per game, that is good for you. They may miss **continuation bets** (the act of following a preflop raise with a bet on the flop), and value bets. They also may not get betting tells on you, or may be too rushed to optimize their play. In particular, I like betting when they miss their continuation bet. If my opponent misses a continuation bet opportunity, the advantage goes to me because I now can bet and maybe win the pot right there. I can also opt for a free card.

The point is that I now have more options than if the player had followed through on his continuation bet.

Multitablers are easier to bluff because they like to get involved with good hands, not marginal ones. You can bluff them off small and medium pots, and get out of the way when the pot gets big—unless you have a big hand, of course. Specifically, they start fewer hands, meaning they generally start with good cards. Consequently, they are less inclined to **defend blinds**— play a raised pot when one is in the big blind (or, less often, the small blind), and not necessarily fold just because one has substandard cards for the situation.

When you do try to take advantage of a multitabler, don't lose sight of the fact that they are frequently good players who tend to know how to maximize the return on their good hands. But also remember that multitablers can't carefully observe their opponents' individual characteristics, and must rely on tracking software. This makes them vulnerable when their opponents deviate from their usual tendencies.

You can and should exploit your multitabling opponents by consciously deviating from your typical play. If you are a tight player, you can play more speculative hands. If you are usually loose, then tighten up and play premium hands.

Review your own statistics and change your patterns against players who are relying on tracking software to play against you.

How to Identify a Multitabler

If you wonder if a player is multitabling, use the "find user" option, which sometimes appears when you right-click on the player. Or you might find it by returning to the lobby and looking under the main menu options. Information is power. All poker sites offer a "find user" option, but on some sites (notably PokerStars) a player can make himself "unfindable," so you can't always rely on the results. You may need to perform this function yourself, for example by surveying all games of the same type and limit.

GENERAL CASH GAME STRATEGY

TIP #15

START WITH BEGINNER STRATEGY

When you first begin play on a site, it is a good idea to start in the play money games to learn how to use the site, how the buttons work, and so on.

Advance slowly to small cash games. Micro stakes are better for learning strategy than the larger games, even if only pennies (literally) are involved. If you skip steps, you may inadvertently pick up bad habits or miss something.

Study. Read the good literature on poker. Look for books that are written and recommended by top professionals. Read *Card Player*; it's the premier poker magazine and has the most complete website. Read the best online advice, but be discriminating while you're doing so. There's an awful lot of information about poker online and a lot of it is bad or outdated.

Play on one site to build up points so that you can take advantage of their promotions.

As to what game to play, I strongly suggest no-limit hold'em because that is the most popular game. If you're going to spend time becoming an expert at something, pick the game in which you can be better than many others almost immediately.

Here are some guidelines to remember when playing against other beginners:

- Almost always when you are check-raised on the river you are beat.

- Seldom do you want to call a giant bet with one pair—even an overpair. This is a common mistake among beginners.

- Don't go crazy on the flop when you have a big hand. **Milk** the hand, that is, bet small or moderately to increase the likelihood of getting a call.

- However important you think **position** is, where you sit in relation to others (the later, the better), it is probably more important.

- When you are in a game with six players or fewer, you should generally raise or fold before the flop if you are first to act. Limping should be reserved for nine- or ten-handed games, and even there it's often not the best option.

TIP #16

MIX IN INTERMEDIATE STRATEGY

- The first tip is to read the beginner strategy. Most of us think we are better than we are.

- Figure out what is and is not working for you. Are you winning or losing at certain games or structures?

- Work on your discipline. Discipline is hard to maintain when you are losing, particularly when those losses are to players who play worse than you. Many players adjust by thinking that if they play worse cards they'll still be able to outplay the weaker opponents. That rarely turns out to be the case.

- Are you using software tools? You need to install and become comfortable using applications like Hold'em Manager and PokerTracker

- If you're having problems, drop down a notch, that is, play at a lower level. Online play can be very profitable even at relatively low levels. For example, you might be a winning player in the $5/$10 no-limit game in your local casino. You might then think that the $2/$4 game on a poker site would be easy pickings for you. But you might be wrong, and instead find yourself losing heavily. Don't let pride get in your way. Try the $1/$2 games, or even 50¢/$1.

- Study.

OTHER CONSIDERATIONS

- Be honest about your **leaks**, the flaws in your play, and work on them.

- Pick your games because of the players, not because you feel like playing that game. The biggest factor in being a winning player is playing against weaker opponents, not playing in a particular form or at particular stakes.

- Learn new games so that you have more choices. Focusing on no-limit hold'em is a great starting point, but if you're doing well you should branch out and try new games. Limit hold'em is very popular and many players who have transitioned from no limit fail to make proper adjustments and demonstrate bad habits acquired in no limit play. Pot-limit Omaha and limit or pot-limit Omaha 8-or-better (high-low split) often attract loose gambling players online. All forms of draw poker— high draw at both limit and pot-limit stakes, 2-7 triple draw, 2-7 no-limit single draw—are often eminently beatable, primarily because many of the participants are inexperienced or play poorly.

- **H.O.R.S.E.** (a game or tournament format in which five forms of poker are played: limit hold'em, Omaha 8-or-better, razz, seven-card high stud, and seven-card high-low stud) and other mixed games offer great opportunities because very few players can play many games well.

TIP #17

ADAPT YOUR PLAY FOR HEADS-UP GAMES

If you look at the high-limit area of hold'em right now at your favorite site, you'll see lots of heads-up tables with one player sitting but not too many that are actually playing. You may wonder why. Well these players are vultures (using that expression in the kindest manner, and mixing a metaphor) waiting for innocent fish to stop by to get eaten up.

Between their notes and tools they know who the weak players are and those are the ones whom they are going to play against, as opposed to playing each other. They will often test an unknown player.

Nowhere else are tools more necessary and obvious than here.

Heads up is for experienced, skilled players and not what I suggest for players of lesser experience and skill levels. However if you want to try it, remember that it favors the aggressive. I recommend the following strategy:

- In no-limit hold'em, on the button you probably want to raise about 80 percent of the time, call 15 percent, and fold 5 percent.

- Reraise off the button with premium hands and fold maybe 20 percent of the time.

- Since your opponent will be pushing, you have to see lots of flops as the blind so you don't get pushed around.

Given these guidelines, you can see that you need to take lots of flops and play from there. That's where it gets tough and that's why heads up is for experts.

If you find a passive player, you are going to win unless you go crazy. (Then again, you might go crazy when the player keeps calling with medium hands and you have to let your hand go.)

MULTITABLE TOURNAMENT STRATEGY

INTRODUCTION

Multitable tournaments are the most popular form of online tournament. As the name says, a **multitable tournament** is one that comprises two or more tables—usually *many* more. Whereas typical brick-and-mortar tournaments have a few hundred entrants, online tournaments regularly host thousands and even tens of thousands. While the largest brick-and-mortar event, the World Championship No-Limit Hold'em event in the World Series of Poker, has had as many as 8,773 entrants, that is unusual and the buy-in is $10,000. Online tournaments regularly have up to tens of thousands of players for buy-ins from $1 to $200.

In these big tournaments, prize pools tend to be very large and players can win large sums for relatively small investments. Because of this, **variance**, the swings in one's bankroll, is high in online tournaments. Players lose sight of online tournament variance and tend to set the wrong goals for themselves.

TIP #18

ONLY AIM FOR THE TOP PLACES IN A TOURNAMENT

If you're going to play tournaments regularly, you must constantly remember that the big money is in the top few places and that prize money increases at an accelerated rate. Consider these facts:

- In a typical online tournament, about 10 percent of the entrants get paid.

- Most players who cash in an online tournament only make a modest profit, sometimes less than doubling their initial buy-in.

- More than half the total payout is usually made at the final table, and the top three finishers generally win about 40 percent of the total prize pool. The payout figures depend on the individual tournament and the number of participants. A $200 Sunday tournament I played had 5,000 players. It finished within twelve hours and paid over half the prize pool to the final nine. Another weekend event had some 60,000 players, lasted nearly fourteen-and-a-half hours, and paid 38 percent of the prize pool to the final table.

Multitable tournaments are all about getting to the final table and having a shot for a big hit. That's it. Nothing else matters if you want to make a big score. One good win is better than just barely making it into the money every time. If you want to be passive and your main goal is just to have a payoff, there are many better online poker options for you. If you can't take the variance either emotionally or financially, play something else or qualify by a method other than paying cash.

If you buy in with your own cash, you must play with the intention of making the final table.

TIP #19

EARLY STAGE TOURNAMENT STRATEGY
—PLAY LIKE A CASH GAME

This section uses no-limit hold'em to illustrate optimal play because most of the giant online tournaments are played in this form. Multitable tournaments typically offer a lot of play early on. Large entry tournaments generally start with deep stacks, often upwards of 300 big blinds per player. In addition, large entry tournaments usually offer twenty minutes or even half an hour of play per level.

Many people, myself included, have a tough time with such a large stack as 300 big blinds because winning a few chips in a small pot doesn't feel like it means much. I used to start play an hour late because of that. In a tournament that is expected to last twelve hours, an hour less of being forced to concentrate is welcome.

However, I have come to learn that there are so many bad players in online tournaments likely to quickly lose their entire stack, that it's too good of an opportunity to pass up. If you come in an hour late, many of these terrible players will already be gone—with their chips usually relocated to the stacks of tougher players.

So try to start playing each tournament from the first hand that is dealt.

- Don't be the complainer swearing on the way out of your online room about your bad luck. Just because you play well, there is no guarantee you're going to win—or even that you will make it past the first break. One of those early wild players may pick up a real hand against your good holding or the player may take the worst of it and draw out on you. To improve your chances of avoiding this fate, don't play a giant pot in a situation that is likely to be a close call.

- Because of these huge-stack-to-blind ratios, the early stages of multitable tournaments play more like cash games than tournaments. Take one hand at a time and make fewer overall mistakes—and for sure fewer *major* mistakes than the others. Other players will be making big mistakes during these early stages, like putting an entire stack in on a weak draw or a single pair. Don't be that player—be that player's opponent instead.

TIP #20

MIDDLE STAGE STRATEGY—
ADJUST BASED ON YOUR STACK AND YOUR IMAGE

As time passes, the average ratio of stack size to big blind amount goes down, antes start, and major differences in players' stack sizes develop. Furthermore, table image starts to come into play.

- Position now becomes much more important. You need better starting cards with multiple players left to act because it costs you more to play, relatively speaking, than in a typical cash game. Conversely, good strategy dictates playing weaker starting hands in later positions since the blinds and antes are worth relatively more and other players are generally more reluctant to call. Of course, you should always keep in mind the tendencies of those that remain to call, particularly the blinds.

- High cards increase in value as fewer players take the flop. And this is typically what happens in the middle stages of online tournaments. People play more wildly in the early stages, slow down in the middle, and step up the looseness—and aggression—in the later stages, particularly when they're **in the money**, having lasted long enough in a tournament to guarantee finishing as one of the winners.

- If you have a big stack, you can test your table bullying possibilities. For example, if you got your big stack because you picked up some big hands and won a few good pots, then players may start to become afraid of you and won't want to play with you with less than a premium hand. Moreover, since their stacks are shorter they may not be *able* to play with you. This is generally a good time to play some more hands and start picking up extra blinds and pots.

- Be aware of your image and use it to your advantage. If your image is weak, don't try tricky plays. If your image is strong, capitalize on that: be aggressive! With a tight image you can steal pots. With a loose image you can check-call some nice pots, because those who perceive you as loose will bet marginal hands. With an aggressive image you can overbet because your opponents will think you are pushing marginal hands and bluffs. With a passive image you can check-call just as you can with a loose image. And since you essentially have no image when you move to a new table, play conservatively and observe until you see how others are playing at your new table. Of course, don't throw away good hands. Just play relatively tighter than usual until you scope out the lay of the land.

TIP #21

GET AGGRESSIVE ON THE BUBBLE

As a tournament reaches its later stages, the *bubble* approaches and play changes. The **bubble** is the position just out of the money in a tournament. For example, if a tournament pays forty places, the player unfortunate enough to bust out in the forty-first position is said to have been **on the bubble**.

Stack sizes—both your own and those of your opponents—are very important at this stage of a tournament. If you have a big stack, do not follow the strategy of backing in to the money as so many people do. That is, don't just coast, playing only premium hands in the hopes that others will clash and bust each other out, allowing you to end up among those receiving a payout.

- Your job is to take advantage of the short stacks who have to play extra tight in order to cash and the weaker players who think there is something magical about getting their money back or making a tiny profit. In most tournaments, the bottom prizes of the payout ladder are often equal in size to the buy-in and the next few levels don't offer much more. As we discussed, the real money is in the top few places.

- As the bubble approaches, the most likely callers of relatively large bets will be very short stacks with a big hand and big stacks who are not afraid to lose a fraction of their holdings.

- With a medium stack against a big-stack bully, you can three-bet with the proper hand even if it might break you. You are trying to get to the final table. If you have to take a risk to get there, better that than settling for a small payout. Because of the previously mentioned variance, you will not make money playing in tournaments by making a number of safe just-in-the-money cashes. Your wins will be farther apart—thus, increased variance—but your overall record will be better by having fewer **cashes** (finishes in the money) as long as those cashes are among the top few places. The best way to have a chance to win a top prize is to take chances. It bears repeating that in this stage of the tournament big stacks will be raising you way lighter than usual, and reraising these players offers you a great opportunity to acquire a large stack yourself while gambling with the best hand.

TIP #22

JUST IN THE MONEY—LOOK FOR EASY TARGETS

If this book does nothing else, let it change your mindset right now. When the bubble has been reached, and thus all those players that remain are guaranteed a payout, the tournament is really only just beginning. Remember that many of those remaining players are those that are satisfied with *any* payout. They are likely to have short stacks and are easy targets, particularly if those around them have large stacks. If you have been playing as I advocate, you are like a PGA golfer who just made the cut and now gets to come back to play for the money.

- Once the survivors reach the money, play loosens up considerably. Do not be one of those players who now, satisfied with having made the money, busts out with a weak hand.

- On the other hand be on the alert for those spots to pick off. They might be the ones who were playing super slow over the last fifteen minutes and begging others to slow down so they can creep into the money. This unattractive behavior is a real clue that the player probably is on **short real money**, not having much actual cash, so he is not playing anything.

TIP #23

FINAL TABLE STRATEGY—GO FOR THE WIN (OR AT LEAST THE TOP THREE PLACES)

When you get to the final table—I hope it's *when*, not *if*—your strategy changes. Things are set. You know the players, the seating assignments, and the final table chip counts. You also know the payout structure, but that will take care of itself. Simply put, the higher you get, the better the payout. You will make an effort to climb higher, or, if you're already high, to ensure you stay there.

You have now played with many of these players for a while but others are new and you have just come off short-handed play. Before the final table was assembled, there was a point at which there were two short-handed tables, with maybe as few as five players at your table. Once the remaining players got down to seventeen, the tables were kept balanced. With ten players remaining, the tables were at five and five until one player busted out. (This applies to tournaments with nine-handed tables. Some tournaments have six-handed tables and some are heads-up tournaments.)

Take stock of things. The table is full and generally players are not in a hurry—except for the few short stacks who feel they have to *move in* soon. To **move in** is to bet all one's chips. At the final table, a player with a short stack feels pressure to get the entire stack into the pot before the blinds and antes completely erode his stack. He hopes to do so with a good hand, but, the shorter the stack the more desperate the player and the lesser the quality of the hand he is likely to have.

If you are a short stack, you do not want to be a caller unless you have a big hand or a stack equal to less than a few big blinds.

- If you have less than ten big blinds, you need to be raising with a pair or decent ace in position while you still have enough chips so that the blinds do not have to automatically call you with any hand. This means that at a nine-handed final table and a stack equal to eight big blinds, you do not want to put all your chips into the pot under the gun with, for example, A♠ 8♣.

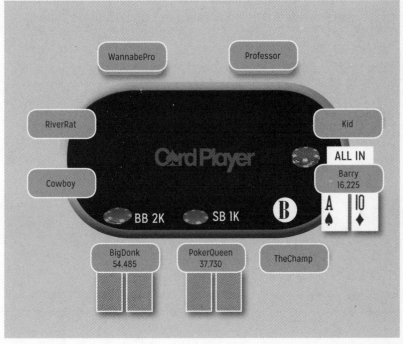

Raising While There's Still Time

- When you have a stack between ten and twenty big blinds it is not panic time. However, you need to look for opportunities to reraise a looser big stack, while still having enough chips to get the original raiser to fold or to double up to a comfortable stack if you are called and win.

- Medium stacks often are hanging around trying to move up a notch or two. That is, they are playing similarly to the way many people play shortly before the bubble, just hoping to survive, playing nothing but premium hands. Some people have a problem with those who adopt such tactics; I don't. I *do* have a problem with observing it and not taking advantage of people acting as if they are just a piece of furniture. Don't become one of these passive medium stacks, and exploit their passivity in return.

TIP #24

AS THE FIELD NARROWS
—FOCUS ON YOUR OPPONENTS' STACK SIZES

As the final table thins out, yet another factor enters your poker strategy thinking. Stack sizes are still very important, but now the payout structure—and your opponents' strategies in relation to this—come to the fore. Consider the following:

- As players drop, you play shorter handed. This means that big cards further increase in value.

- If the opposition still includes crazies (kamikaze players or maniacs who lucked into the final table), it is a good time to wait. But more often the better players tend to be left and they deserve respect.

- Big stacks can kill you even if those holding them are crazy.

- Middle stacks are the most conservative. They are the ones to go after. This is because they can't just call indiscriminately as the big stacks can, since a big stack usually has to call only a relatively small portion of his stack. And they don't feel the imminent pressure that the little stacks feel.

- Small stacks are a target because they can't hurt you in the way the medium and big stacks can, but realize that they may not fold as easily.

- Big stacks are a good target too if you can play with them cheaply and in position in case you outflop them. It's easier to trap someone if you act after him. When you're first to act, if you plan a check-raise, he may just check behind you. If you overbet your good hand, he may just fold.

- If your opponents are generally folding in an attempt to move up, you need to exploit them by stealing some pots.

- If others are playing aggressively, you need to be more patient. If you have a big stack, then you can be more passive than the aggressive players but more aggressive than normal.

- If you are the chip leader, you probably already know to try to get control without being crazy. You can do one of the following:

  - Control pot size by calling bets (as opposed to raising)

  - Decide whether to raise small or big

  - Three- or four-bet with big hands

My personal preference is to let others knock themselves out early before becoming more active. Until you develop your own style, and of course it depends on the situation, this might be a good tactic to adopt.

Heads up strategy in a multitable tournament is consistent with cash game heads up strategy discussed before.

MULTITABLE TOURNAMENT STRATEGY: MORE TIPS

TIP #25

PLAY YOUR TABLE, NOT THE OTHERS

Your job is to focus. It's that simple. So focus on your opponents and on your own play at your table. However, it is important to know how close to the money you are because of how play changes as the bubble approaches and again, once everyone is in the money, so keep an eye on the tournament lobby.

If you are new to online tournaments with large fields, you may be concerned about beating so many players. But that's not your worry. Your job is to increase your stack size against the nine players at your table. The other tables will take care of themselves.

TIP #26

CONCENTRATE ON THE MOMENT AND BE PATIENT

You cannot win without aggregating every chip in the tournament. Nevertheless, a multitable tournament is not a speed race. Forget about making the money. Remember, the point at which all participants are in the money is when the tournament really starts. So just concentrate on the moment.

If about 15 percent of the players get paid, then when you get into the money the average stack will be about seven times bigger than what you started with. Play your stack accordingly.

TIP #27

STAY AWAY FROM TRAP HANDS

Hands like A-10 or K-J are trap hands. That is, they might win a little or they might lose a lot. If they improve, it's often to a "good enough" hand that may cost you a lot. With hands like these, the worst case usually is that you flop top pair and lose many or all of your chips to a better hand.

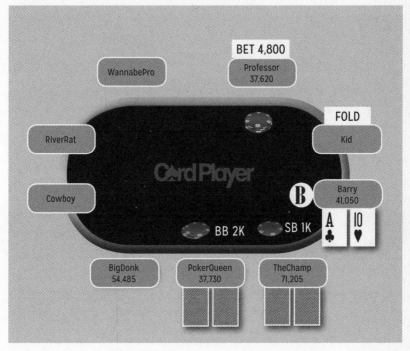

Watch Out!

An unsuited weak ace is another hand that invites trouble. Barry's gift—I give you permission to fold **A-x** (an ace with a small card) in the big blind when only one other person entered the pot for a raise.

It depends on the situation, of course, but, in general, you're not giving up a lot by not playing this hand out of position against one opponent and you may well save a lot.

TIP #28

STUDY CAREFULLY AFTER YOU MOVE TABLES

I mentioned this earlier, but it bears repeating. When you get moved to a new table, it is important to take extra care to learn the table. See where the **speed** is—if someone shows a lot of speed, he bets and raises aggressively; if someone doesn't have a lot of speed, he plays passively—who is the bully, where passivity is located, etc. Read your notes if you have information on the other players.

Don't start by playing hands that are close calls. You must educate yourself to how your new opponents play before inadvertently giving a lot of chips to the resident rock.

TIP #29

TAKE CARE OF YOUR EYES AND YOUR BRAIN

Old guys like me need to use breaks to rustle up stamina. You young bucks can do as you please. Sitting for hours in a poker tournament takes staying power and focus. That comes easier to young people. Also, looking away from the computer while playing is important.

Eye doctors recommend gazing off into the distance every ten minutes for at least a few seconds to reduce eyestrain. It will also help your brain.

TIP #30

MANAGE YOUR BANKROLL CAREFULLY

The big tournaments are where the big wins are and they aren't played just by experts, so you ought to be playing them, too. But if you don't have the funds to enter tournaments with relatively large buy-ins (although tournaments with big prize pools often have reasonable buy-ins online), use *satellite tournaments* to get your entry and use these satellites as practice too.

A **satellite tournament** is one in which prizes are buy-ins into larger tournaments (as opposed to cash prizes).

TIP #31

AVOID GOING BROKE WITH TROUBLE HANDS

Generally you don't want to be busting out of a tournament with any of the following hands. Of course, it always depends on the situation. If you're in a pot with a maniac who seems determined to give away his chips, some of these holdings might be worth gambling with. Otherwise, don't call off your stack with these:

- Ace-king all in preflop. It might be okay to put your stack in as the raiser or call if you are very short, of course. And before you do put everything at risk, ask yourself if your opponent would put his net worth into the pot on a **coin flip**—any confrontation of two closely matched hands, such as two overcards against a pair in hold'em before the flop. The reality of tournaments is that you often have to participate in a coin flip for your tournament life, and ace-king is a good hand to do that with, but don't just decide to make the call automatically.

- High pair that is outflopped.

- Drawing hands—A beautiful flush draw (four-flush) looks good but connects only about 1 in 3 if flopped and 1 in 5 on the turn.

- Overpairs (or top pair with top kicker) when reraised.

- Any hand when check-raised on the river.

- Any hand where the opponent looks like he hit the lottery (oops that's for live action.)

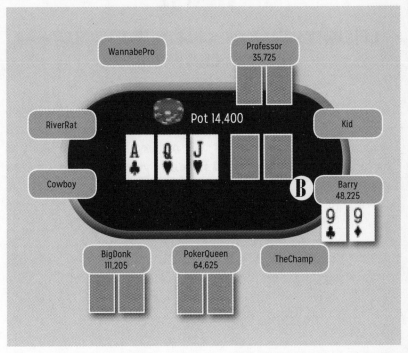

My hand's probably not good anymore

- Ace-queen when three-bet behind you. However, it's true that light three-, four-, and five-betting is prevalent now in online tournaments, so your notes on a particular player may indicate that you should reraise sometimes. In general I like ditching ace-queen out of position, but I know many players don't easily give up on the hand.

TIP #32

CALL WITH SOME GOOD NON-PREMIUM HANDS UNDER THE RIGHT CIRCUMSTANCES

Certain hands are worth a call with, even if the pot has been raised, as long as that call is not for a large portion of your stack and if the other players who are involved (or are likely to be involved) have large stacks. This is very dependent on your stack size. Calling a raise when you have a very big stack is fine if you still can win lots if you outflop the raiser. Just be careful about improving at the same time as the opponent does.

- Small pairs if you can bust a decent-sized stack by flopping a set

- Suited connectors with plenty of players

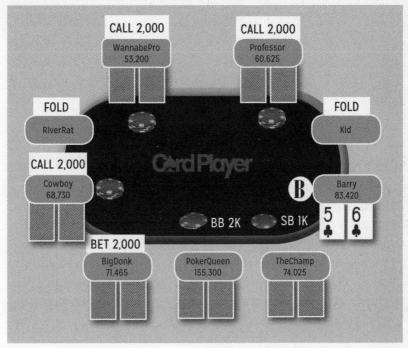

Good spot to play suited connectors cheaply

- Anything in late position against somebody who will check-fold the flop if he does not improve

Be careful with all of these oddball hands against great players. The reason is they can get away from a hand and you won't get your value out of them if you hit.

TIP #33

MANUFACTURE HANDS WHEN YOU NEED TO

Because the blinds keep moving up you must make some aggressive plays sometimes. If you just can't catch a hand you must manufacture one. This is easy to say, of course, but it's tough to execute (and, unfortunately, tough to teach), so don't be in a hurry to do it. Don't be ashamed of getting caught in a play either. Great players show down some junk hands. Sometimes a play works; other times it looks silly.

But don't be embarrassed if the play looks silly if you did it for a well thought-out reason. Just pick your spots very carefully. A good time is when rainbow low cards hit the flop.

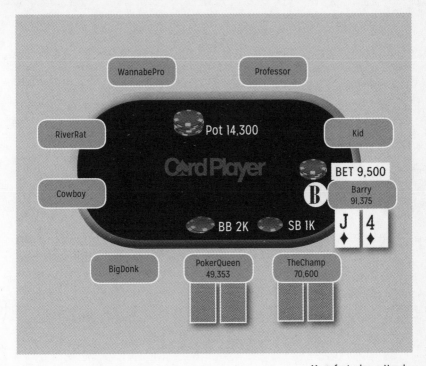

Manufacturing a Hand

TIP #34

DON'T BE PREDICTABLE
(EXCEPT FOR BEING PREDICTABLY TOUGH)

You should be predictable in that you are tough and people are afraid of you. You do not want to be so predictable that they know what you are holding.

TIP #35

BE AGGRESSIVE WHEN BLIND-VERSUS-BLIND

When the pot hasn't yet been opened the small blind generally should raise with a decent hand in an effort to take the pot uncontested. "Decent" here means high cards, medium to high suited connectors, any pair, and the like. It doesn't mean low cards, unless the big blind is particularly timid.

The big blind should reraise when he thinks he has a *dominating hand* or when he thinks the small blind is too aggressive with his raises. A **dominating hand** is a hand that is significantly ahead of another, usually because of having the same card in common plus a higher card.

TIP #36

BEAT THE ROCKS

One principle that works well playing online poker tournaments is that if you can beat A-A, A-K, or K-K when playing a rock, you should be ready to commit all your chips. If you flop a set or make two pair on the turn, you will usually have the best hand against a rock. This is because rocks only play the best cards. They will not be in pots with J-9 or 6-4. Unlike maniacs, you will not have to worry about them holding random cards that beat you.

A maniac gambling with random cards will outdraw you a lot more than a solid rock will. But the rock will often stubbornly call with that big hand that has been outdrawn.

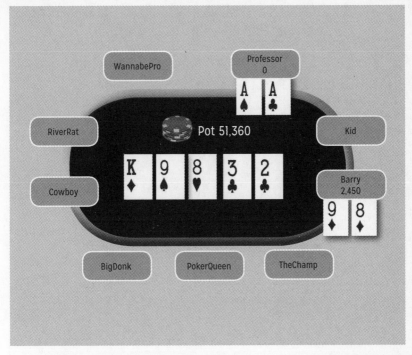

Beat the Rock

MULTITABLE TOURNAMENT STRATEGY SUMMARY

Multitable tournaments take time, and you must be prepared to give them your full concentration for the entire event. That is, winners are rewarded by playing their best game all the time. That means:

- Accumulate chips a bit at a time as the opportunities present themselves.

- Don't be in a hurry.

- Let the others dump their chips off.

- Bet when you have an edge.

- Bluff with discretion when it looks like the other player may be weak (but not as weak as you).

- These tournaments take hours and you will have some bad luck. Do not tilt.

- Remember, the tournament is really just starting when you make the money.

MULTITABLE TURBO TOURNAMENT STRATEGY

INTRODUCTION

If you love online multitable tournaments but don't have ten hours to play, **multitable turbo tournaments**, a multitable online tournament that has quickly accelerating limits, may be perfect for you.

Multitable turbo tournaments have been described as tournaments on crack because the blinds increase so rapidly. Therefore many assume they are just luck. This is simply not true. As in other forms of poker, there are decisions to be made and those who make the best decisions win more.

Actually it might be more accurate to say that those who make the *fewest poor decisions* win more in the long run.

You get the same number of chips as in regular tournaments (bigger buy-ins may get more chips, just as they do in regular tournaments) but levels are faster, often consisting of five-minute rounds. Even with high buy-ins, the blinds will be very high compared to the size of the average chip stack within an hour.

- Because of the shorter levels, there will be more short-term variance in your outcome. If you can't stand the many losses you may have to endure before having a profitable upswing, turbos are not for you.

- Players generally do not react to the shorter levels or, maybe even more often, overreact or react incorrectly. This makes for lucrative opportunities.

- You won't be needing and shouldn't be trying many **cute plays**—sophisticated plays, such as check-raising and slow-playing, designed to outplay the opposition. Winning tournaments is all about getting in with the best of it. The preferable situation is that you be the raiser and not the caller so that you have two ways to win, as opposed to the one way you get when calling. The two ways are your opponent can fold or you can win at the showdown.

- Just waiting for the nuts will kill you. Look for weaker players to exploit with good hands—or sometimes even bad hands.

- A turbo will have lots of all-in coin flip hands. You must win them to win the tournament. This is one of the main reasons for the higher variance at this type of tournament.

- You can be smart by not always playing for all your chips. Towards the end of any turbo tournament all but the biggest stacks are forced to go all in because of the blinds being so high. Try to feel out your opponents and figure out if they are big gamblers (maniacs) or if they are supertight (rocks) and make your decisions accordingly.

- Players who continually push all in throughout the entire turbo tournament rarely win. If they do, it's because they were extremely lucky. Crazy constant raisers usually lose because people realize what they're doing and wait to pick them off. If they happen to have a good hand when someone has picked up what he thinks is enough to catch them or if that's the time they make the straight, then they pick up a lot of chips and the "trapper" might bust out.

- Take control of your hands by always making smart logical decisions. Your opponents may think you're pushing marginal hands (and you may be). Let players move all in on you all the time and when you finally pick up a **monster**, a big hand for a situation, your patience will pay off. That is, if you play selectively aggressive and find yourself winning the hands uncontested preflop, then if you pick up or flop a big hand you may induce players behind to move in on you.

TIP #37

EARLY STAGE STRATEGY—PLAY SOLIDLY

In theory since the payouts, chips, and blind structure at early levels are similar to regular multitable tournaments, early strategy should be the same. For the most part that is true. However my experience is that players tend to be in even more of a rush to go broke and play crazy in turbos. That argues for playing more marginal hands cheaply in position and low pairs cheaply from all positions.

- Even though you want to avoid risking your chips early, it may be worth it if you are up against an overly aggressive player whom you may have dominated.

- There is no need to try to push someone off a hand with garbage. Much more often *they* will be pushing to try to double up. Also, trying to pick up just a couple of chips early doesn't do much for you. You are looking to double up, too. The way to do it is to start with the best hand and then get their chips. Depending on your opponent, the best hand often doesn't have to be nearly as strong as in a regular multitable tournament.

TIP #38

MIDDLE STAGE STRATEGY—BE THE AGGRESSOR

The middle of a turbo comes quickly. That means blinds start getting big relative to the average stack size.

- Be extra careful with your starting hand because you will be playing fewer hands total than in normal tournaments.

- You must push more often with good hands and be prepared to make more calls.

- Try to be the aggressor—not the caller—unless your hand is very big.

- As in other tournaments, passivity is not rewarded, but maniacs are your friends, even if they **suck out**—beat someone's hand when behind by catching one or more cards for improvement—on you periodically.

A prevailing theory, espoused by many pros is that if a *standard raise* preflop takes at least a third of your stack then you must go all in. In a no-limit game, a **standard raise** preflop is coming in for (usually) two-and-a-half to three or four times the size of the big blind.

I disagree with this premise for two reasons:

- You can lay it down against an all-in reraise if you "know" you are beat. This might be based on your notes.

- You may still be *pot committed* and yet have a better chance of winning by **shoving** (going all in) on the flop rather than preflop. **Pot committed** is being in a situation in which a player is likely to see the pot through to the end because the amount of chips he has left is relatively small compared to the amount already committed to a pot or compared to the current size of the pot. Your opponent may fold if his medium-strength cards didn't hit the flop, while there is a much better chance he would call before the flop. Also, you might hit the flop yourself.

At this point of the tournament, most hands are won or are all in by the turn.

TIP #39

LATE STAGE STRATEGY—BE THE RAISER, NOT THE CALLER

The late stage of a turbo also comes quickly. At this point blinds are big relative to the average stack size.

Here is where you need a balancing act. You can't win without being aggressive, yet I think at this stage many more players tend to get overly aggressive rather than play too passively.

- As usual, you want to be the raiser to have two ways to win (they fold or you have the best at showdown).

- Calling raises with small pairs is way overrated in these tournaments, particularly late. The reason is if you are dominated (pair over pair) you have only one chance in eight of outflopping the other player. That is great early in the tournament or when just risking a small amount. That is terrible if you don't have much to win from the opponent. And if he doesn't have you dominated, then you probably have a coin flip at best. You'll be in many coin flip situations, but better to be in as raiser than caller.

- The same (calling raises) can be said for **ace-little** (an ace with a small card); it is often a bad play.

- You must push more often with good hands and be prepared for more calls.

- Again, be the aggressor not the caller, unless your hand is very big.

- Sometimes just hanging around for an orbit or two ratchets you up quite a bit in the standings. That is, late in the tournament, because of the tendency toward overaggressiveness by most players, just patiently awaiting decent cards may improve your standing as the others knock themselves out.

- Final table strategy is similar to that of multitable tournaments, but varies according to buy-in. Larger buy-ins tend to have stacks with a larger ratio of stack size to big blind than smaller buy-ins, which provides more maneuverability. If you have twenty-five to thirty big blinds in your stack, there is no rush. But if you have fifteen big blinds, faster play, that is, being more aggressive with marginal hands, is necessary.

SUMMARY

Turbos are faster than regular multitable tournaments. That means you must play more aggressively than in the latter. Just don't overdo it.

Just as in every tournament, you have to focus on the game and make good decisions. But perhaps the most important point is that those who make the *fewest poor decisions* win more in the long run.

SIT-AND-GO STRATEGY

INTRODUCTION

Sit-and-gos ("**SNGs**") are usually one-table tournaments that start when players have sat and the table is full. **Multitable SNGs** are just like scheduled multitable tournaments, except that they start when all the tables are filled instead of at a set time, therefore you should refer to my multitable tournament strategy when playing multitable SNGs. The strategy in this section applies only to single table sit-and-gos.

SNGs are good for several reasons:

- It's easy to get a game. Just sit down and wait for the table to fill. That often happens in minutes or even seconds. Or jump into a table that is beginning to fill.

- You can play for almost any stakes. Buy-ins range from hundreds and even thousands of dollars down to $1 or less. You can even find free entry SNGs with prizes of cash or entries into real money SNGs. Poker sites also offer SNGs with frequent player point buy-ins that award cash prizes and entries into major tournaments.

- SNGs allow you to practice all the tactics you have been mastering. Played right, they combine the table selection of ring games with the final table play of multi-table tournaments. That is, you can select your

91

opponents in ring games and you can select them to some extent in SNGs, something you can't do in multi-table tournaments, where you're subject to the luck of the draw. You also get to play as if you were at the final table of a multi-table tournament, giving you much-needed practice that you might otherwise be hard-pressed to find. You can jump into an SNG anytime; making the final table of a tournament is no easy task.

TIP #40

CHOOSE THE RIGHT SNG

Much of the strategy for SNGs is the same as for all poker games.

- Pick worse players, if possible. If you have color-coded players that you have played with before, you can look for them at SNG tables that are just starting up. Software is also available that finds the softest games—easiest to beat because of the weakness of the opponents—for you.

- If you can, choose your seat relative to opponents whose playing styles you know. Generally you want the toughest opponents and the maniacs to your right, and you want the weak and predictable players to your left. You want the tough players to your right so you know what they're doing before you have to act and you can stay out of their way. You want the maniacs there so you can isolate them or, failing that, know that you will be less at risk of losing all your chips. You want the others to your left because you don't have to worry about what they're going to do; they're not likely to make surprising or unpredictable moves.

- Make notes for those players you don't already have notes on—and update your notes as needed while the

SNG progresses. Players sometimes play differently on different occasions, and your earlier observations may have been skewed or erroneous. They'll be at your table the entire tournament, so get to know them. Know, for example, who seems afraid; this might allow you to snag some blinds.

The three preceding points are very important and yet often overlooked even by decent players. One more thing to keep in mind:

Buy-Ins

Often the size of the buy-in dictates the length of play, which may be relevant. That is, bigger buy-ins frequently start out with more chips or more time per level or both.

TIP #41

GENERAL STRATEGY: SHOOT FOR THE WIN

The speed of level change and stack size have strategy implications you can tailor to your preferences. These influence the time the SNG lasts in the same way as normal, **deep stack** (a starting chip stack whose ratio of the size of the starting stack to the big blind is large compared to a "normal" tournament), and turbo tournaments. Do yourself a favor and make life easier by playing where you have the biggest advantage. That is the surest path to profit.

- Do not play stakes too high for either your bankroll or comfort. You do not want to be making poor decisions out of fear.

- Low buy-in SNGs are a good place to practice tournament structures that are not currently your best. In an SNG, you'll experience everything from full table to heads up—and all stages in between. Just heed this warning, though. Buying in too often at low levels, events in which the cash for first doesn't mean much to you, probably also means that you will not have the patience and discipline to play your best and win.

- SNGs are good for practicing short-handed play. An SNG bears some similarity to the final table of a multitable tournament in that both have an ever declining number of players. It is different in that the chip count is different. In an SNG, everybody has the same starting chip count. It would be unusual for the final table of a multitable tournament to begin with all equal stacks, or even stacks close in size. Nonetheless, if you play a lot of SNGs, you'll find yourself often in situations that are the same as those that arise in multitable tournaments. And they all come down to the same thing: heads up.

- As for multitabling, you can do so with SNGs just as any other games, but this is definitely not my first choice. It's harder to play an SNG by formula than a ring game. SNGs have a much greater necessity to observe the players at the table and how they are playing *right now*.

- As in other tournaments, just making the money is not your goal. When you have made the money is the point at which the tournament really starts.

- Don't get nervous if one player starts out accumulating lots of chips. Let him break the ones who do panic while you move up steadily.

- Here's a mathematical concept that many fail to grasp. It is true for *all* tournaments, but easiest to explain for SNGs. The usual payout is in a ratio of 50:30:20. (For example, if the buy-in is $10, the prize pool would be $90, paid out $45 for first, $27 for second, and $18 for third. (This neglects the house take, which for a $10 SNG might be $1 per player, making the actual buy-in $11.) Once the three finalists are in the money, 60 percent of the money they will split is accounted for. Each winner is guaranteed to get at least 20 percent. The other 40 percent is paid out this way: Nothing goes to third, 10% to second, and 30% to first. This is figured as 20-20 (which equals 0), 30-20 (10), and 50-20 (30). The difference is huge. The incremental money (what a player stands to make by not finishing third) for first is three times second. So play to win. That is where the money is.

TIP #42

EARLY STRATEGY—PLAY TIGHT

Early in an SNG, play tight, tight, tight. Let others knock themselves out. If possible, play as few hands as needed—perhaps only three or four—just to back into the money. And, as we have seen, since that's when a tournament really starts, that's when you can really start playing. Perhaps that extreme is too much of a stretch, but just ask yourself this question: *Do I need to play this hand?*

- In early position, play only premium hands (and I mean high pairs and A-K). In late position, you can add a few more hands like middle pairs (9-9 and 10-10) or A-Q. Let me reiterate, your play in the early stages should be very tight.

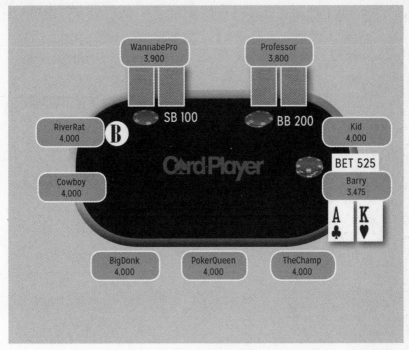

Early Position Aggression Early in a Sit-and-Go

- Early play means thinking of both how many blinds your stack represents and also how many players are left. People tend to think too much about where they stand compared to the average stack and not enough about how many big blinds their stack consists of. Also, every time somebody gets knocked out you can play a wider range of hands.

- Position is still important at all levels.

- If you can get in cheaply in late position, you can add to the hands you play—two suited face cards, suited aces with a middle kicker (A-8 suited would be playable, for example) and higher, and all pairs.

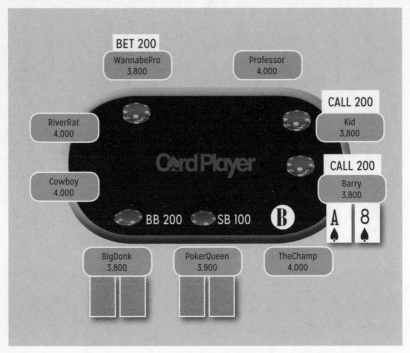

Late Position Speculation Early in a Sit-and-Go

- Don't bluff in the early stages of an SNG. Or at least only bluff rarely. Everything depends on situations, so you can never say never in poker.

- Don't chase postflop. That is, if you flop a draw and it looks like it's going to be expensive to continue, give up.

- Do make continuation bets.

TIP #43

MIDDLE STRATEGY—CHANGE GEARS

The middle of an SNG is the time to change gears. The blinds come around faster, but even if this is not so (because players haven't busted out as quickly as expected), they have gone up three or more times and the average stack is considerably smaller in relation to the blinds than it was earlier.

- This dictates a need to start picking up blinds—in position. Position is extremely important here.

- Bluff a bit, judiciously. Again, in position. Know who seems likely to fold and who not, and proceed accordingly.

- You will find great *semi-bluffing* opportunities in late position. **Semi-bluffing** is a bet made on a hand that is probably not the best at the time of the bet, but that has a possibility of improving to the best (that is, has one or more outs).

- Many people are ultra tight when just out of the money. Pick on them. Steal their blinds unmercifully. Semi-bluff. If your stack is relatively large, push against them.

- Don't worry about drawing hands against you. Yes, your opponents will play them and they will get there sometimes, but it won't often be the multiway pots that make drawing to such a hand the right play. So if they play such hands, they're making mistakes and you will profit from the mistakes your opponents make. The corollary from this is that, of course, generally you shouldn't be playing with a drawing hand.

- If you can't find hands then you must manufacture them (see "Multitable Tournaments" chapter) against people who are reluctant to call or at least in position. Even though you should play fewer hands in a sit-and-go than in other formats, you still can't win if you get **blinded off**, lose the blinds each round by staying inactive (not playing hands) until your chips eventually trickle away completely.

TIP #44

IN THE MONEY—INCREASE THE PRESSURE

The final three players in a sit-and-go get paid. When the fourth player busts out, the rest are in the money. Just as in every other tournament, profiting in an SNG is about winning, not just reaching the money. Tournament structures, including SNGs, favor the top, and that argues for aggression. Since an SNG is such a small tournament, in this case profit comes from winning, or occasionally coming in second. You won't profit if you're continually shooting for third place because you won't make that often enough to pay your entries.

- One of your mantras should be to pick on the weak.

- Once you are in the money, notice—and do this quickly or base it on your notes—the players who seem to be relieved to have made the money and suddenly switch from playing nothing to playing everything. Catch one of them and you'll be heads up.

- By now you should know your players. The concentration required to get this knowledge is difficult to sustain when multitabling. This is why I don't like multitabling SNGs.

- If you find yourself with ten big blinds or less, make a play. Try to be first to act when you make the play so you have two ways to win (opponents fold or you have or make the best hand). You don't always have a choice, but if you do, try to be the shover not the caller.

- With a big stack, keep up the pressure. Don't just lie down and let others catch up. Put in many—but smallish—raises preflop, and continuation bets.

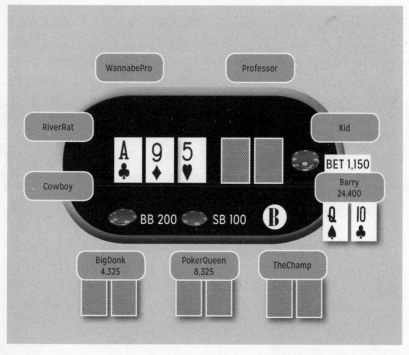

Keep up the Pressure with a Big Stack

- If you get to heads up, it is the same as explained previously.

- If you are often finishing in second place, then you probably need to adjust by adding more aggression to your heads-up game. Also, if your opponent is overly aggressive, then wait a bit to move in on him and hopefully pick him off.

SUMMARY

- Play tight early.

- Be more aggressive as blinds go up and the field gets smaller.

- Make the money half the time, and first place half of that time, to feel good about your play.

HYPER-TURBO STRATEGY

INTRODUCTION

A **hyper-turbo**, also known as a **super-turbo**, is a very speedy version of a single table SNG.

Each player usually starts with only ten big blinds; for example, if the blinds start at 15/30, players begin with 300 chips. The blinds increase every three minutes and there is no **time bank**—an aggregated amount of time upon which a player can draw when he exceeds the allotted time for his action. Because of this, someone goes all in nearly every hand right from the beginning of the tournament.

This causes many people to think there is almost no skill involved. But, as in any other form of poker, skill wins out in the long run. Hyper-turbos have high variance, higher even than turbos, but they only take thirty minutes or so for a winner to emerge. They may take a lot less time if you don't make it that far! On average, you may only play ten to fifteen minutes, during which you get lots of opportunities to increase your stack.

As in all tournaments, selective aggression is rewarded.

TIP #45

STRATEGY—PLAY YOUR GAME AND DON'T PANIC

Don't panic about starting with just ten big blinds. Because everyone else is in the same situation, you can wait until you're down to five big blinds to push (go all in) and maybe half the field will be gone.

- You prefer two ways to win, that is, you want to be the raiser not the caller, so you might win by getting the opponent to fold or by having or flopping the best hand. Otherwise you would like to have the raiser dominated, so you need an extra strong hand to call. It is a poker truism that you need a better hand to call a raise with than what you would yourself raise with. Be prepared to go all in with big pairs and A-K. It is okay not to call with middle pairs and even A-J. A-Q is iffy; playing or not playing might depend on your notes.

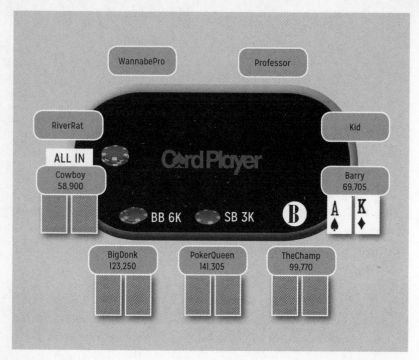

Go All In with A-K

- The maniacs still lose in this form of tournament, just not quite as often due to the higher effect of variance and the greater part that short-term luck plays. That's fine. Pick them off.

- **Stop and go**, a play in which a player bets into an opponent who has previously raised or otherwise shown aggression, can be effective in hyper-turbos because draws often won't call and the flop is missed 70 percent of the time. Thus, a hand that might have been willing to go all in before the flop (if the player raised and you reraised) might well fold on the flop.

- If you find yourself in good shape (double the average stack size) early, you can start putting pressure on the others, especially in late position. That is, you should be more aggressive than in ordinary tournaments and even more aggressive than in turbos. This is especially true when approaching the bubble.

- Be extra aggressive against very short stacks who cannot hurt you.

- One writer has suggested not to lose any big hands in hyper-turbos. That's a good idea in theory, but if you play ultra passively you have zero chance of winning tournaments in general, particularly ones with a fast structure, such as turbos and hyper-turbos.

- In fact, in hyper-turbos you must get all your chips in when you are the raiser and in position with hands in which you might have just a 60/40 lead (or less!), for example, a hand like K♦ 10♦, which is about 58-to-42 against Q♠ J♠. The same goes for any coin flip situation—get your chips in the middle as the raiser.

- As the clock ticks down, so does the size of your stack relative to the big blind. It moves fast; you cannot wait for monsters. Pairs and high cards have extra value because drawing hands like 8-7 suited won't have the value that they do in slower tournaments. In the latter arena, the bet size relative to your stack might be smaller and the number of participants might be greater. This combination rarely happens in hyper-turbos, but your opponents will still be playing those hands.

- Often king high will take down the pot, especially as the field narrows. Be prepared for wild swings.

SUMMARY

- In a hyper-turbo, you must be aggressive, but it is better to do so as the raiser or reraiser and not the caller. If you must be the caller, try to do so with good cards.

- Don't feel pressure to make a move until you get down to five big blinds or less.

TOOLS AND TRAINING

TIP #46

USE SOFTWARE TOOLS AND ONLINE TRAINING

As we saw earlier, you must use tools to win the most you can as an online player. You might still be able to become a winning player without them, but you won't do nearly as well as you might otherwise. Your savvier opponents have tools and with those tools they know a lot about how you play. You need your own tools to level the playing field.

And to become that winning player, you will benefit from training. Both tools and training are available online, naturally enough.

CardPlayer.com offers four applications to help with your game. They are found at http://www.cardplayer.com/poker-tools.

TIP #47

PLAY WITH POKER ODDS CALCULATORS

Card Player's hold'em odds calculator is the most popular one on the Internet. You just input any two or more hands and learn how they fare against each other. You can start preflop and learn your exact chances of winning on any given hand. Alternately, you can specify the flop or turn. Find out just how much of a bad beat you suffered or whether you made a good call.

Simply click on cards to get percentages on the fly. Find out how your odds look preflop, on the flop, and after the turn. The calculator also works for Omaha and Omaha 8-or-better.

TIP #48

READ POKER HAND MATCHUPS

Turn to *Card Player's* Hand Matchups to relive the biggest pots and most interesting hands from the world's largest poker tournaments. Hand Matchups recount all of the crucial poker hands from World Series of Poker events, including those of the WSOP main event final table, and from other world-class tournaments.

Each hand also includes an analytical breakdown of each play, putting some perspective on whether Daniel Negreanu made the right laydown or whether Phil Hellmuth's tirade about how badly his opponent played was justified.

TIP #49

INPUT ALL OF YOUR RESULTS INTO POKER STATS TRACKER

Track your online and live poker results for free with the Poker Stats Tracker. This application lets you keep track of every single penny you win or lose playing poker and provides charts, graphs, and statistics for tournaments and cash games. You can even filter your results by: buy-in, stakes, cardroom, game type, or pretty much anything else.

Best of all, it's accessible anywhere you can access the Internet— and did I mention that it's free?

TIP #50

USE HOLD'EM MANAGER WHEN YOU PLAY ONLINE

Card Player strongly recommends Hold'em Manager. Find it at http://www.cardplayer.com/poker-training/hold'emmanager. You can try it out for free before buying.

Hold'em Manager offers:

- The ability to replay hands with current historical stats

- A Heads Up Display (HUD) with customizable popups

- Multiple stats, displaying profitable situational stats

- Mucked display that shows opponents' **mucked cards**, cards thrown away unshown but, since part of a called hand, available to hand histories.

- Unlimited database size

There is also an Omaha Manager, which supports both the high-only version and the 8-or-better (split pot) version.

You'll find both products at http://www.cardplayer.com/poker-training. Since they really are tools, we list them in this section.

TIP #51

SIGN UP FOR ONLINE TRAINING

You learn from the ground up by taking an online training course. And if you already play a decent game, you can get to be a much better player with one. Many courses are out there, and it's hard to tell the good from the bad. Seven of the best video training courses available are at http://www.cardplayer.com/poker-training:

BlueFirePoker (http://www.cardplayer.com/poker-training/bluefirepoker) brings you videos from pros who crush the games. BlueFirePoker makes it a point to feature only the top players.

CardRunners (http://www.cardplayer.com/poker-training/cardrunners) is the world's largest poker training website with over 2,000 poker videos, hundreds of poker blogs, and active strategy forums.

DeucesCracked (http://www.cardplayer.com/poker-training/deucescracked) helps beginning players start winning, intermediate players become advanced, and advanced players become unstoppable.

TournamentPokeredge.com (http://www.cardplayer.com/poker-training/tournamentpokeredge) focuses exclusively on MTTs with top ranked players such as bigdogpckt5s. With no sign-up fee and the lowest monthly charge it can help you start winning tournaments today.

DragTheBar (http://www.cardplayer.com/poker-training/dragthebar) is a full-featured training site that offers cutting-edge strategy from some of the biggest winners in the games today.

At **Deepstacks University** (http://www.cardplayer.com/poker-training/deepstacks), you're placed at a virtual poker table with some of the world's best poker players in Team Deepstacks.

Card Player **Pro** (by PokerSavvy Plus; http://www.cardplayer.com/poker-training/cardplayerpro)) focuses on multi-table tournaments, Sit 'n' Gos, and no-limit hold'em cash game instruction from some of the most profitable online poker players.

FINAL TIP

TIP #52

NEVER STOP IMPROVING YOUR GAME, EVEN IF YOU ARE WINNING.

GLOSSARY

This glossary contains only those terms that might not be familiar to all readers. If you've played any poker, you already know what holdem is, what a bet or raise is, and what straights and flushes are, so terms like those do not appear.

Cross-references are <u>underlined</u>.

Many terms are adapted from *The Official Dictionary of Poker* and used with permission.

ace-little: An ace with a small card.

aggressive: Pertaining to a style of play characterized by much betting, raising, and reraising. This is not the same as loose play. Some of the best players are very selective about the cards they play, but when they do get into a pot, play those cards aggressively. Sometimes subcategorized as *loose-aggressive* and *tight-aggressive*.

all-in protection: In online poker, a facility that prevents a player's hand from being folded when the player loses his Internet connection. If the player gets disconnected, the player is all in for the amount that has been bet up till that point and a side pot is created for any further action. If the player has the best hand at the showdown, he receives the main pot. All-in protection is usually offered only in limit games. No-limit and pot-limit games are generally designated as not having all-in protection.

A-x: An ace with another card, probably a small card, with "small" meaning 9 or smaller.

badugi: Four-card triple-draw ace-to-five lowball with suited cards being equivalent to pairs. The best hand is A-2-3-4 of four different suits. K-Q-J-10 is better than an A-2-3-4 that has two cards of the same suit. The game is sometimes one of the offerings in a <u>mixed game</u>.

berry patch: A game full of weak players, one that is easy to beat.

bet slider: See <u>slider</u>.

blinded off: In a tournament, if you don't participate in any pots, or participate in only a very few, you lose the blinds each round until your chips eventually trickle away completely. This situation is called being *blinded off*.

bonus: Online cardrooms offer first-time players incentives, called buy-in bonuses, such as a "gift" of up to $1,000 to match the player's initial deposit. Bonuses have to be earned back in the same way as FPPs are awarded, that is, a certain amount is allocated for each raked pot in which the player participates, until the entire bonus is earned. Sometimes a bonus is awarded only in a lump sum when fully earned; other times, bonus money is released as increments are earned, such as $100 at a time for some percentage of the necessary accumulation of points. Similarly, a *reload bonus* is periodically offered to regular players, in which, upon reloading (making a new deposit), some certain amount, usually a fraction of the amount deposited, is awarded, to be released in the same manner.

brick-and-mortar cardroom: A cardroom with a physical presence, as opposed to online. The term is often shortened, particularly in print, to *B&M*.

bubble: The position just out of the money in a tournament.

buy-in bonus: See bonus.

calling station: A weak player who rarely raises, but calls almost every bet, even with substandard hands (and hence should not be bluffed).

cash: In the context of a tournament, to cash means to finish in the money, that is, in one of the paying places. As a noun, a *cash* means such a finish.

check boxes: Controls that permit a player to select a play (check or fold, and, in limit games, bet, raise, raise any, etc.) before it is his turn to act. The software waits to implement the action until it is the player's turn to act. When the application implements the function as radio buttons, they are often known as *advance action buttons*.

clean outs: See outs.

coin flip: Any confrontation of two closely matched hands, such as two overcards against a pair in hold'em before the flop. For example, the confrontation 4♥ 4♠ against K♠ Q♣ gives an expected value of 52.5% for the pair and 47.5% for the overcards. That is close enough to 50-50 to be called a *coin flip*.

continuation bet: In hold'em, the act of following a preflop raise with a bet on the flop, or, sometimes, a flop bet with a bet on the turn. Sometimes shortened to *c-bet*.

cute plays: Trying to outplay the opposition with sophisticated plays, such as check-raising, slow-playing (checking or underbetting big hands), making a large reraise with a drawing hand, and the like. Also called *fancy play syndrome*.

deep stack: In a *deep stack tournament*, a deep stack is a starting chip stack (what you have on the table when the tournament starts) whose ratio of the size of the starting stack to the big blind is large compared to a "normal" tournament. Deep stacks are common in the larger multitable tournaments.

deep stack tournament: See deep stack.

defend a blind: Play a raised pot when one is in the big blind (or, less often, the small blind), and not necessarily fold just because one has substandard cards for the situation. It's harder to bluff a player who regularly defends his blind.

dominating hand: In hold'em, a hand that is significantly ahead of another, usually because of having the same card in common plus a higher card. For example, ace-king dominates king-queen. Similarly, a higher pair dominates any lower pair.

draw out: See <u>suck out</u>.

8-or-better: In a split-pot game, the specification that a hand can win the low half only by having five different cards ranked 8 or lower. Seven-card stud and Omaha have variants in which the pot is split between the holder of the highest hand and the holder of the lowest hand. If no hand qualifies for low, the high hand wins the entire pot.

forced-move game: See <u>must-move game</u>.

fast structure: Describing a tournament in which chip stacks are relatively small compared to the size of the big blind and levels are shorter than generally found in tournaments.

forced-move game: See <u>must-move game</u>.

FPPs: See <u>frequent player points</u>.

free card: In hold'em, the situation in which there is no bet on a particular round, so players get extra cards without having had to risk additional money. For example, you are on the button with A♠ Q♠ in a pot you raised or reraised. The flop is 2♠ 7♠ J♦, giving you four to the nut flush. An early player bets, and one player calls. You raise, and both call. No matter the turn card, the other players may check to you. If another spade doesn't come, you can check also, allowing you to see the river card for "free."

frequent player points: Incentives offered to players by an online cardroom to keep the players loyal to the site. These are awarded in the form of points allotted at some predefined rate per number of raked hands (those from which the house cut, or drop, has been taken) played, and stored as part of a player's account. These points can be redeemed for cash, merchandise, and entry into tournaments. The term is often shortened to *FPP* or *FPPs*, particularly in print.

full-bet rule: See <u>half-bet rule</u>.

half-bet rule: Specifies what constitutes a legal raise. A legal raise is one that can reopen the betting, that is, allow those that have called only the unraised bet to now reraise. This comes into play when a player goes all in. In some cardrooms, an all-in raise of half or more of the preceding bet or raise can now be reraised; in others, only an all-in raise equal to or more than the preceding bet or raise reopens the betting. (The latter is called the *full-bet rule*.) For example, in a game with blinds of $5 and $10, Emilie comes in for $25. John and Chloe call. Matt raises to $100. Andy goes all in for $150. Paul calls that $150. Emilie, John and, Chloe fold. If the half-bet rule is in force, Matt can reraise, because Andy's all-in bet constituted a legal raise. If the full-bet rule is in force, Matt can only call. The half-bet rule is the usual case in online cardrooms, whereas in B&Ms the full-bet rule is more common.

hand history: A virtual replay of one or more previously played hands. At some online cardrooms, a hand history appears as a textual or graphical summary of the hand that can be viewed online while playing upon the conclusion of the hand; at others, it is sent to the requesting player as an email message. Most cardrooms offer both options.

heads-up display: Overlay software that displays hand history statistics directly onto an online poker table. The statistics are usually obtained by a data-mining utility, and are sold by a company not associated with any poker site for use by online players to give them knowledge of their opponents' historical tendencies. Some sites allow the use of heads up displays, others do not. Often shortened to *HUD*. Also see tracking software.

H.O.R.S.E. A game or tournament format in which five forms of poker are played in rotation, usually one round of each. The games are limit hold'em, Omaha 8-or-better, razz (seven-card lowball stud), seven-card stud (high), and seven-card stud high-low (the *E* standing for 8-or-better). H.O.R.SE. is a mixed game.

HUD: See heads-up display.

hyper-turbo: A speedy version of a multitable turbo tournament, one with smaller starting stacks, in which blinds usually go up every three minutes, and with no time bank.

in the money: Having lasted long enough in a tournament to guarantee finishing as one of the winners (that is, those that get paid; all other entrants receive nothing for their efforts). Usually 10% to 20% of the field is paid in an online tournament.

isolate: To isolate a particular player is to bet in such a way (usually by raising or reraising enough to make it difficult for others to come into the pot) as to end up heads up (one on one) against a particular player.

leaks: Flaws in your play.

limp: Open the pot on the first round of betting for the minimum, that is, an amount equal in size to the big blind. When players limp, the big blind has the option of not raising, thus ending the wagering for that round, or raising, and reopening the betting (that is, allowing anyone who has already called to call the raise or reraise).

lobby: Main view into an online cardroom, the primary source of information about all the games available on the site, containing a summary of every game.

milk: Bet small or moderately to increase the likelihood of getting a call.

min raise: Raise the minimum. For example, if the blinds are $5 and $10, to min raise is to open the pot for $20 rather than some higher amount. As a noun, it means a raise of the minimum.

mixed game: A game or tournament format in which several different games are played in rotation, usually one round of each. H.O.R.S.E. is an example.

monster: 1. The nuts, that is the best possible hand at the moment (or close to the best when the best possible is unlikely.) **2.** A big hand for a situation, not necessarily the nuts or even a particularly great hand. Flopping two pair in hold'em against one opponent could be a monster depending on the situation.

move in: Bet all one's chips.

MTT: See <u>multitable tournament</u>.

muck: Throw away one's cards, generally without showing anyone those cards.

mucked cards: Cards thrown away unshown. On the river, if part of a called hand, available to hand histories.

multitable tournament: A tournament with more than one table, and usually many more than just a few. The term is often shortened to *MTT*, particularly in print.

multitable turbo tournament: A <u>turbo tournament</u> with more than one table.

multitabling: Playing at more than one table at a time. You can't do that in a B&M, but online you just open more windows, each representing another table. Multitablers typically play at four to eight tables simultaneously, while some play as many as twenty-four.

must-move game: A must-move or forced-move game is the second game of its type at a specific limit in a public cardroom that acts as a feeder to the main game, according to rules that vary from cardroom to cardroom. As seats become available in the main game, players in the forced-move game must move to the main game. The reason to have forced-move games is to make sure that the main game is always full, as opposed to the *balanced-game* situation in which two tables might both have vacancies, and yet no one is permitted to change games until one has at least two more open seats than the other.

nosebleed limits: Very large cash games.

on tilt: Playing poorly and irrationally due to emotional upset, often caused by the player in question having had a good hand beat by an opponent who had way the worst of it by having played vastly inferior starting cards (often in complete disregard of the odds and good play) or the player having lost a pot because of his own bad play. The term comes from pinball, in which a machine, if shaken too violently by a player to influence the path of the silver ball, stops functioning and its front panel displays the word "tilt."

orbit: Once around the table, with respect to dealt hands, that is, one opportunity for each player to have the button and each of the blinds.

outs: Cards that improve a hand, usually used with reference to a hand that is not currently the best hand. The term is most often used for hold'em, but can be used for stud or Omaha, and sometimes even draw games. For example, in hold'em you have A♠ 8♠, an opponent has 2♥ 2♣, and the board shows 2♦ J♠ Q♠ 9♦. Any 10 gives you a straight, and any spade gives you a flush. Four 10s remain, and nine spades. One of those spades, 10♠, was already accounted for among the 10s. Two of the spades that make you a flush also improve the three 2s to four of a kind (2♠) or a full house (9♠); thus, you have ten outs. In a case like the preceding in which some of the apparent outs (which you might count if you didn't know your opponent's holdings), those outs that unquestionably would give you a winner no matter the opponent's holdings are called <u>clean outs</u>.

overbet: Bet more than you think would be called by a typical player or more than the situation calls for. Against a <u>calling station</u>, there's a good chance your bet will be called.

position: Where you sit in relation to others. If you sit behind (act after) the only other player in a particular pot, you have *good position* on him. (Sometimes the wording is shortened to *you have position on him*.) If you sit on or near the button, you have position on the others at the table.

pot-committed: Being in a situation in which a player is very likely to see the pot through to the end, no matter the cost, generally because the amount of chips he has left is relatively small compared to how much he has already committed to a pot or compared to the current size of the pot. For example, in no-limit hold'em, particularly in a tournament, the phrase often is heard to describe someone who has already called or bet half or more of his stack.

probe bet: In a no-limit game, a small bet made to see if anyone will raise or to determine who will just call.

push: 1. See <u>shove</u>. **2.** Play aggressively, particularly when part of the phrase "push someone off [a hand]."

qualifier: The specification of what a hand must consist of to win the (usually) low half of a split-pot game. See <u>8-or-better</u>.

razz: Seven-card stud in which the lowest hand wins. The game has no <u>qualifier</u>

reload bonus: See <u>bonus</u>.

reopen the betting: Start a new series of raises within a betting round. That is, a player has already called the initial bet, there has been a raise, and another player could end the round of betting by calling the raise, but the player instead chooses to reraise. For example, in a hold'em game, three players limp, including the small blind. The big blind raises, and the first two limpers call that raise. The small blind could call, which would *stop the betting*, or he could choose to reraise, and *reopen the betting*.

ring game: Any game played for "real" chips or cash, that is, specifically not a tournament game.

rock: An extremely tight (conservative) player who generally stays in only on premium cards.

satellite tournament: A tournament whose prizes are buy-ins into larger tournaments. For example, a $75 single-table satellite might award a buy-in to a $500 tournament for first place, with perhaps cash for second and third places. Satellites can, and often do, have multiple tables, in which case multiple entries are usually awarded.

semi-bluff: A bet made on a hand that is probably not the best at the time of the bet, but that has a possibility of improving to the best (has one or more <u>outs</u>). If the bet gets everyone else to fold, it succeeds as a bluff; if it does not, the hand might still improve. For example, in hold'em, if a player has 5♠ 6♠ and the board is K♠ Q♠ 4♥ and bets out, if no one has anything, the bettor might win the pot right there. If anyone calls, though, which a player with a king or queen in the hole undoubtedly would do, the bettor is behind, but could still win if another spade appears on the turn or river.

short real money: Not having much actual cash. A player in the middle stages of a tournament may have borrowed the money to get in or won his way in via a satellite, but, if he busts out, he'll have to scrape to get the buy-in for a game.

shove: Go all in, often as the first better in a particular round, sometimes as the raiser. The term usually does not apply to *calling* all in. Also, *push*.

sit-and-go: A special (usually) one-table tournament that starts as soon as a full table of players are seated. So called because you sit down at an empty (virtual) seat in such a tournament and wait for the table to fill. Online cardrooms also offer multiple-table versions that start when as many tables as are designated fill. The term is often shortened to *SNG*.

slider: In an online no-limit or pot-limit game, a control that lets players adjust the sizes of their bets. You click and drag to operate the control, usually moving it to the right to increase the bet or raise. In a pot-limit game, the slider range is from the minimum bet to the size of the pot, while in a no-limit game, the only constraint to the upper range is the size of your stack.

SNG: See sit-and-go.

soft: Said (usually) of a game, easy to beat because of the weakness of the opponents.

speed: The relative liveliness of a game, whether the players are acting aggressively, passively, or somewhere in between. The term also applies to individual players. If someone *shows a lot of speed*, he bets and raises aggressively. If someone *doesn't have a lot of speed*, he mostly folds against aggressive play and doesn't himself bet large or raise much.

standard raise: In a no-limit game, coming in for (usually) 2.5 to three or four times the size of the big blind.

stop-and-go play: A play in which a player bets into an opponent who has previously raised or otherwise shown aggression. For example, in a hold'em game, on the flop, Emilie bets into John, John raises, and Emilie just calls. On the turn, Emilie bets into John again. Emilie has just executed a *stop-and-go play*. Often shortened to simply *stop-and-go*.

suck out: Beat someone's hand when behind by catching one or more cards for improvement, as, making a straight or flush against a high pair or a set or by catching the third card to a small pair against a higher pair or two pair; often followed by *on*. "I had him on the flop and turn, but he sucked out." Also sometimes called *draw out*.

tell: A mannerism that gives away your holdings. In B&Ms, typical tells include smiling when you have a big (very good) hand. More subtle tells include iris dilation, a throbbing pulse, or acting in a certain manner in a given situation. Since you can't see those things in your online opponents, you may think that tells do not exist online. They do, as this book explains.

three-bet: Reraise, that is, raise someone who has initiated the betting with a raise.

tilt: See <u>on tilt</u>.

time bank: An aggregated amount of time upon which a player can draw when he exceeds the allotted time for his action. This concept is most prevalent particularly in tournaments, although it is also used to limit player time allotments in ring games, in which only a short time is given for each action. For example, a player might have a one-minute time bank. He might be allowed 10 seconds for any action. If he exceeds those 10 seconds for whatever reason, then any additional time is subtracted from the time bank. When the time bank is depleted, the player must act upon the current hand immediately (and any succeeding hand within the allotted time) or his cards become dead. If the allotted time is exceeded because the player's connection to the website was dropped or otherwise compromised, some online cardrooms give an automatic extension and do not subtract from the time bank. Time banks are also used in some televised poker tournaments. Time banks are specifically not used in <u>super turbos</u>.

tool: Third-party <u>tracking software</u>.

tough: In a poker context, tough means difficult to beat, not hard to play.

tough player: A very good or successful poker player, one who is thus difficult to beat.

tournament trail: The yearly cycle of major poker tournaments, including the World Series of Poker, European Poker Tour, World Poker Tour, and the *Card Player* Poker Tour, but also including others such as the National Championship of Poker at Hollywood Park Casino in Inglewood, California, and the PaddyPower Irish Open at the Burlington Hotel in Dublin.

tracking software: Applications that keep track of the hands you and your opponents played, and provide you with that information in summary form, showing you, for example, how often a particular opponent raises or reraises with particular hands, what percentage of flops the opponent sees, and so on. These database applications are usually sold by companies not affiliated with any particular poker site. The results are often shown in a <u>heads-up display</u>.

turbo tournament: An online tournament that has quickly accelerating limits. Where in an ordinary tournament the limits may go up every 15 minutes, in a turbo tournament they might go up every five minutes. The level sizes are usually the same as regular tournaments; the difference is the speed, thus the name. The name is often shortened to simply *turbo*.

value bet: Bet a hand with the intention of getting called by a lesser hand, as opposed to getting the other to fold. Value betting usually implies betting a hand that has only a slight edge, and one that a conservative player would likely check with.

variance: Basically, this refers to the swings in one's fortunes while playing. If you graph your wins, the more erratic the path, the higher the variance. As it pertains to tournaments, your bankroll generally fluctuates radically. You may go long periods without a win (a long downward slope in the graph line) and then suddenly a big win might cause a spike that (you hope) brings your bankroll into positive territory.

GREAT CARDOZA POKER BOOKS
ADD THESE TO YOUR LIBRARY - ORDER NOW!

DANIEL NEGREANU'S POWER HOLD'EM STRATEGY *by Daniel Negreanu.* This power-packed book on beating no-limit hold'em is one of the three most influential poker books ever written. Negreanu headlines a collection of young great players—Todd Brunson, David Williams. Erick Lindgren, Evelyn Ng and Paul Wasicka—who share their insider professional moves and winning secrets. You'll learn about short-handed and heads-up play, high-limit cash games, a powerful beginner's strategy to neutralize pro players, and how to mix up your play, bluff and win big pots. The centerpiece, however, is Negreanu's powerful and revolutionary small ball strategy. You'll learn how to play hold'em with cards you never would have played before—and with fantastic results. The preflop, flop, turn and river will never look the same again. A must-have! 520 pages, $34.95.

POKER WIZARDS *by Warwick Dunnett.* In the tradition of Super System, an exclusive collection of champions and superstars have been brought together to share their strategies, insights, and tactics for winning big money at poker, specifically no-limit hold'em tournaments. This is priceless advice from players who individually have each made millions of dollars in tournaments, and collectively, have won more than 20 WSOP bracelets, two WSOP main events, 100 major tournaments and $50 million in tournament winnings! Featuring Daniel Negreanu, Dan Harrington, Marcel Luske, Kathy Liebert, Mike Sexton, Mel Judah, Marc Salem, T.J Cloutier and Chris "Jesus" Ferguson. This must-read book is a goldmine for all serious players, aspiring pros, and future champions! 352 pgs, $19.95.

SUPER SYSTEM *by Doyle Brunson.* This classic book is considered by the pros to be the best book ever written on poker! Jam-packed with advanced strategies, theories, tactics and money-making techniques, no serious poker player can afford to be without this hard-hitting information. Includes fifty pages of the most precise poker statistics ever published. Features chapters written by poker's biggest superstars, such as Dave Sklansky, Mike Caro, Chip Reese, Joey Hawthorne, Bobby Baldwin, and Doyle. Essential strategies, advanced play, and no-nonsense winning advice on making money at 7-card stud (razz, high-low split, cards speak, and declare), draw poker, lowball, and hold'em (limit and no-limit). This is a must-read for any serious poker player. 628 pages, $29.95.

SUPER SYSTEM 2 *by Doyle Brunson.* SS2 expands upon the original with more games and professional secrets from the best in the world. New revision includes Phil Hellmuth Jr. along with superstar contributors Daniel Negreanu, winner of multiple WSOP gold bracelets and 2004 Poker Player of the Year; Lyle Berman, 3-time WSOP gold bracelet winner, founder of the World Poker Tour, and super-high stakes cash player; Bobby Baldwin, 1978 World Champion; Johnny Chan, 2-time World Champion and 10-time WSOP bracelet winner; Mike Caro, poker's greatest researcher, theorist, and instructor; Jennifer Harman, the world's top female player and one of ten best overall; Todd Brunson, winner of more than 20 tournaments; and Crandell Addington, no-limit hold'em legend. 704 pgs, $29.95.

CARO'S BOOK OF POKER TELLS *by Mike Caro.* One of the ten greatest books written on poker, this must-have book should be in every player's library. If you're serious about winning, you'll realize that most of the profit comes from being able to read your opponents. Caro reveals the secrets of interpreting *tells*—physical reactions that reveal information about a player's cards—such as shrugs, sighs, shaky hands, eye contact, and many more. Learn when opponents are bluffing, when they aren't and why—based solely on their mannerisms. Over 170 photos of players in action and play-by-play examples show the actual tells. These powerful ideas will give you the decisive edge. 320 pages, $24.95.

Order now at 1-800-577-WINS or go online to: www.cardozabooks.com